The Swerve

JULITH JEDAMUS was born in Boulder, Colorado. A novelist and editor, she has lived in London for sixteen years.

T0290275

JULITH JEDAMUS

The Swerve

CARCANET

First published in Great Britain in 2012 by
Carcanet Press Limited
Alliance House
Cross Street
Manchester M2 7AQ

www.carcanet.co.uk

A CIP catalogue record for this book is available from the British Library

ISBN 978 1 84777 134 6

The publisher acknowledges financial assistance from Arts Council England

Supported by
ARTS COUNCIL
ENGLAND

Typeset by XL Publishing Services, Tiverton
Printed and bound in England by SRP Ltd, Exeter

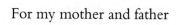

For my mother and father

Acknowledgements

Some of these poems have appeared in *New Poetries V* (Carcanet, 2012), *New Walk*, *The New Yorker*, *The North*, *PN Review*, and *The Tablet*.

My editors, Michael Schmidt and Judith Willson, have been invaluable from the very start, when the first poem was read and the first cover images discovered. I owe a great debt, too, to the many people who have given me their support and critical advice. You know who you are: I shall be thanking you privately. I am also grateful to that marvellous dusty warren known as the London Library, where I, and the books I was searching for, were rescued from obscurity time and time again by its helpful staff – all of whom seem to possess an uncanny sense of direction.

Contents

The White Cliff

This is the face of England, sheer and plain,
the book read backwards, the sugar-loaf,
the main, the high plucked forehead of a queen,
the cracked wall of a citadel. Half
of me believed this, and half did not,
as I walked its furzy crown one night
in June, the metaphoric rock beneath my feet
felt, not seen, and cliffs to the west bright
as lace, festooned with fissures and gaudy
similes. At sunrise, a gull rose above the face,
and I wished for its literal eyes – and I thought of
my rebellious ancestors, who left this place
for a more austere one. After they had gone,
the cliffs, unconscious, shone and shone...

Belle Tout

Beautiful, futile: a flash, then darkness. Cliff-
bound, cliff-threatened, your housed light
drenched in cloud, your minatory face half-
seen, half-guessed: what's this, that
led men not to safety but their graves?
Silent siren, beacon to the dreaming drowned,
who could have guessed your motive? Lives
were your trophy. Below, waves wound
themselves on the shingle, and white cliffs rise,
cancelling your beauty. How fortunate when,
a century past your founding, you were prised
from the cliff-edge and moved inland, drawn
on oiled rails. Now, blind and disarmed,
you guard the green endangered downs.

Bob-Mill

Down the dean they came, on skim-milk
mornings, shadows darkening ponds,
breath rising through beeches, talk
            tumbling, hands
numb, thumbs thick as thimbles. Down
clough and beck they came to the blazing mill.
Twelve hours they worked in its din,
weaving Confederate cotton, shuttle and spool
rattling like the clatter of their days
and their close-clipped lives.
Children past childhood, makers of graves
            and fustians, who grieves
for you now as you walk home in the dark,
your clog-irons ghosting a path of sparks?

The White Horse

What is this broken body? Flesh
dissolves, bones fill green charnels,
      blood's washed
into grooves and channels.
White runnels run. They are a kind
of rune. Who can read this poem?
The grooves suggest only themselves, and wind
that scours them is its own conundrum. No one
remembers the battles fought here. Yet
      the creature persists. Stand on
a ridge, or fly hawk-high, and see her great
palled eye, her double nostril, her forelegs flung
in flight, her arching neck, her haunches braced
against the grass, her harrowed grace.

Rievaulx I: The Abbey

Such audacity! To move the River Rye,
to harvest souls and fleeces, to mine
psalms and iron, to build these high
crossed towers in the northern
wilderness...
        Where is your limestone Eden,
your stronghold of love? The white militias
are disbanded; the lead roofs and golden
caskets have been sintered to arm treasonous
armies. Green enclosures lie open;
crows span broken clerestories; the illumined
world has turned to coal. Plunderers find
a flagon of wild strawberries. In recent rain,
stone basins fill near mossy crevices
where abbots dried the feet of novices.

Rievaulx II: Aelred

Who can read your mind, absent friend,
defender of solitary sisters and fraternal love,
griever for the weak-willed, saver of men
and brimming rivers? No one tried to save
        you. How eagerly you left
the world for your parchment army;
        how you craved the double heft
of prayer and power. Yet your strengths, to me,
convince less than your weaknesses: the affairs
of your youth, your doting letters to desirous
friends, the plunges into baths and rivers
never cold enough to purge your desires.
In your last lean years, your body parched
as frozen linen, you couldn't bear to be touched.

The Lucombe Oak

It was an accident, this cross-bred tree,
this evergreen error that stands its ground
improbably, having survived two centuries
of wind and lightning. Its singular parent, found
by chance in a garden in Devon, is dead now –
killed by the man who loved its gnarled
limbs and bronze-cast crown.
A hundred feet tall it stood, his frail
colossus, until he felled it – and saved the boards
for his coffin. By the time he died they'd rotted.
Does this tree recall that vanity? Listen: the wood's
creaking. They're falling, love: the knotted
arms, snapped knees and elbows. It is no lesson,
this tree. But still, love, listen… Listen.

E.T. in the Isère

Edward, the roads here cut through *terre calcaire*:
flints glint on the paths that rise
to combes and cols. The slopes of the Bois Noir
glitter with beeches whose leaves disguise
old injuries: the knife-graze of lovers,
blaze of axe or lightning. What figure
would you find in their scars? What wide
river of words might have flowed from Arras and your
surviving self to make the resin of this wood
palpable? Feather of cirrus and yarrow, sloe-
stain and nettle-sting, black boars
rooting for walnuts, crows writing slow
circles over corn or carrion: no beauty's
too slight, no fear too deep to escape your notice.

The Cull

Last night I heard gunshots in Richmond Park,
but my November mind, thick with smoke
    and fear of wars
and phantom men, mistook the reason:
the cull of bucks and stags after the rutting season,
    when mast is scarce.

At dawn I walked through Bog Gate, and found
nothing: no drag mark, no blood on the ground,
    no trace of violence.
Mist threaded red bracken, and the broken ridge
of pollard oaks that march towards Holly Lodge
    and its sharp defence.

By the track they call Deane's Lane I saw him:
a twelve-point stag, his scraped horns trimmed
    with moss and bracken,
his hindquarters lean, one shin gored and clotted.
I watched him browse for chestnuts, and waited
    for a quickening, an unseen sign –
    his, the day's, mine.

Henry Moore's Mother

All his life the sensation stayed
with him, of flesh and bone giving and resisting.
Verde di Prato, elm, lignum vitae,
box, alabaster, travertine:
in these he found his recumbent women, while she
lay unmade, pale in crepe and lace,
in the parlour. He bent and kissed her marble face.

Impossible to paint the night at night.
So he memorised it, rowing out
with the Greaves boy towards Battersea Reach,
hovering in the channel, moth-oars flickering,
as he blindly sketched warehouses,
docks, chimney stacks, derelict
rigs and bridges, smudges of smoke
or mist, stippled stars, reflections.

Then, in lucid morning, he'd mix his 'sauce' –
pigments cut with linseed, thin as Béarnaise –
and spread it on unprimed canvas.
Stain on stain, the scene fixed in his mind
appeared again, bodied and simplified,
its japanned reticence pleasing to him
if not his enemies. He softened brushes over a flame,
flicked details on, propped the picture in Chelsea sun.

'The chimneys aren't straight,' the Greaves boy said.
'But they are Whistler's,' he replied,
rolling another cigarette. Sun-splayed like cats
they smoked, under sprays of wisteria,
their faces shaded by wide low-crowned hats.
They breakfasted – buckwheat cakes and bacon,
a bottle of Moselle – and strolled down Cheyne Walk,
yellow ties flashing like his signal butterflies.

At nine, they rowed to Cremorne Gardens
to watch the spectacles: aeronauts in captive
balloons, tigers and waltzers, shills and freaks,
adulterous couples in supper boxes. *Voici
le soir charmant, ami du criminel…*
The spell held them. Madder lakes spread
across Prussian skies, fireworks blazed,
sparks fell and settled on the mind's canvas.

On the Fast Train from Cambridge to London, Second Class, No A/C, Nine Tunnels

'To the fens and back again'
goes the sleepless mind's refrain...

Fields of rape and fields of wheat:
undulating patterns meet

sprays of hawthorn arching down
hills and verges till we drown

in May sweetness redolent
of the body's cold content

and endless – black! Darkness, quick,
tunnels into minds still flecked

with petals... Pressure, subtle,
riddles the ear, wheels rattle,

pale faces ride palest glass –
Blast of air and light... We pass

blurred stations... Names assemble
in mind's shadow, sprays tremble,

blossoms fall until all
is mingled: what's wrecked, what's still

intact. We pass grim flats,
Emirates, graffiti threats...

King's Cross. Other trains reverse –
or are *we* moving backwards?

Papers flutter, legs uncross,
hands reach for what's not yet lost.

Epiphany

Standing on the stage, eight
at waists, waiting to lower
the boat to December water,
we saw a shape float

past, eddying east
towards the thinning haze,
the water so bright our eyes
deceived us, and thought it just

an object of fun.
'A croc!' gasped the Aussie
stroke. 'No, it's Nessie!'
mocked the bow-man,

and we laughed as it lazed
past. The riggers glinted,
and I flinched, and saw it: the dented
face, river-bruised

and blackened, the cavernous
eye… The cox cried out,
and we threw the boat
just as the River Police

swept past, klaxon
blaring. As we gated the blades
and took our places,
we saw them drag the man

aboard, and we pushed off
with a collective shudder, and rowed,
half-balanced, towards
Hammersmith Bridge. We left

at eight, the tide on the ebb,
the water tinted like wine,
our nerves loosening
as our fingers warmed.

By the time we returned,
oars scraping the shingle,
sunlight angled
towards our gay and reddened

faces, we were glad
to have forgotten him, almost.
An hour later, as I crossed
under the bridge, its shade

doubly cold on that cold day,
I saw a policewoman,
hard-eyed and glum,
standing guard over a gaudy

body-bag, its harlequin
pattern of blue and green
lending a marine
festivity to the occasion.

And I tried, as I walked past,
not to see the face
inside it. Those eyes!
Dark in darkness he lay, past

my understanding and his.
So I left him, the river's
Balthasar – his only birth
his death, if birth it was,

his only gift our blithe
contrary spirits.

Fine Boat

She's thin,
just biddable,
a singular letter
bound for nowhere,
a featherless quill
unstable as air.
She's glair
on glazed water,
the fine line
between flying
and drowning.
How to guide her
past danger's swell
when she's peril
itself? I'd turn
swan to master
her, flaring
arms to wings,
feet to webs,
mouth to beak.
I'd be pure
scull, white
shell and carapace.
Fear's chitin
will harden me
to insect's tunic,
goddess's frock.
My brittle bow
will devour
green waves
as I watch
the ravelling wake.
Do I dream,
or is that my name
spun in cunning
flourishes?

Stowing a Single in Furnivall Boathouse on the Chiswick Mall

in memory of A.J.H.

Andy, I still see
you hoisting the Swift
onto your shoulder,
balancing it up
the ramp, pausing at
the tide-boards, swinging
one long leg over,
then the other – your
Aigles streaked with mud,
your bare knees steady –
crossing the pavement,
nudging the bow-ball
through the bright green doors,
angling the single
up to the rack – breath
held as you eased its
riggers round – stowing
it safely, glancing
at me with your pale
startling eyes, never
mentioning my fears
or mistakes, simply
saying, in your off-
hand way, 'Cup of tea?
Put the kettle on,
and I'll grab our blades.'

The Drowning of Drenthe

I travelled to a level land
Past sleeping towns with names of sand:
     Now they are gone.

The polders from the marshes won,
The houses made of brick, not stone:
     Raise no alarm.

The linseed mill with icy arms,
The whitewashed churches purged of charms
     Evade our look.

The beeches smooth as vellum books,
The storks and blackbirds, doves and rooks
     Are rare as rare.

The coffee urns, the *huis-vrouw* cheer,
The biscuits furled like the New Year:
     The guests are late.

Bronze dagger, pin and carcanet,
Twice-strangled girl rescued from peat
     Bright waves obscure.

The tower wet with widows' tears,
The lion gasping in his lair
     Cannot be traced.

I hear the cries from each high place
As it rose up, victorious:
     The rampant sea.

The past is new, the future old;
Who can say now what rhymes are told
     In this drowned world?

Van Gogh in Drenthe

He walks the cinder path, head crooked, oil-coat flapping,
boots soaked from yesterday's storm, canvas and campstool
under one arm. Pockets stuffed with tobacco and chalk, paint-tubes
rattling in a rain-streaked box. He stops, scents colour as a hound
scents fox. Draws a grid, stabs at his palette, scolds staring
turf-cutters. Works for hours. Forgets to eat. Breathes the immense
autumn twilight, its seriousness. He's one of the watchers. He sees:

Rood: Brick ovens in russet orchards. Glow of peat, smear
of sunrise. A girl's shawl. His bloodshot eyes (he bathes them in tea).

Groen: Drenched grass. Cottages roofed with moss. Near Zweeloo,
inland seas of winter wheat. He feels himself take root:

Zwart of earth, of wet bark, of a crepe-wrapped headdress worn
by a Frisian widow, of locks and wharves, and peat-barges drawn

by white horses. *Blank* canals and fields of hail, pallid faces
of weed-burners and potato-diggers, hands knotting bleached laces.

Grijs: Skies of grey and palest lilac, their iridescence
subtler than oil; light unrenderable, its deliquescence

visible and invisible, merging with mist and rain. High clouds
ravelling between azure gleams – *Hemelsblauw*.

Geel: Candles indoors, lanterns without, comforts shunned, gold
flowers not yet seen, letters still unwritten – the last blood-soiled.

Love-Sonnet to a Rock in Bohuslän

To have come so far, abandoned by glaciers,
        to have met, in this granite
            archipelago, my ice-floe
                heart, to part
from the red-berried *rönn*, the emerald ash and elm,
        to stand at the edge of land
            and consciousness, a kist
                for my heart... Part not
from me. Open your porphyry door, and let
        me rest in the lumen, your deepest core,
            as whales breach off Valön, reach
                here as rumour, or rumour of rumour,
            and waves break on the black
                Skaggerak.

Dommaring

Four thousand solstices
since you were burnt here, at the centre
of the Dommaring, where standing stones
(twenty-two snapped bones)
mark the place where you were left with your glass
beaker, reindeer
comb and whetstone.

Blue fjords
recede; salmon swim among stalks
of rye. Bronze bells, or their echoes, break on rocks
once lapped by the sea. Did you see them, the quartz-
carved rocks glistening with summer springs?
The old violence, the old songs:
from prows and cliffs, men sound their lurhorns.

Where is the soul's measure?
Eighty years since you were plundered like treasure,
weighed against scant evidence, sifted and strained.
Moss mutes your rage,
spent as the word-hoard that whet your features,
lent you mood and motive. A sound
pierces the wood, and this page:

your name, the last rhyme
of the Dommaring.

Osage Orange

Would you like it, he asked, the bow
my father made? We were sitting
in the dark, spars of the Northern
Cross above us, stars quickening
as granite lost its heat, half-moon
low in the east. Nighthawks falling
with their cries, stir of pines, the porch-
swing creaking. My father giving
away his possessions, having
sold the land, the house, the horses –
       my past and his.

I remembered it: a relic
shut up in a box in the tack-
house, never bent, never casting
its arrows, their traces safe in
the tall tin quiver. A havoc
of meteors fell near Vega.
We watched them fade, and I said,
with a quick intake of breath, 'Yes.'
'I'm glad.' I half-sensed his smile. 'Not
that I thought you'd do otherwise.
       But even so…

I'll fletch the arrows, and restring
the bow. Strong linen twine he used,
I still have the spool.' I saw it
there on a bench in the cellar,
a secular taper gleaming
in the cool half-darkness. Surely
the threads had rotted… Never mind,
I thought. Let him do as he likes.
Cut the twine, string the nocks, tighten
the strands, show the art wasn't lost –
       not quite, not yet.

'What kind of wood was it made from?
The bow, I mean.' 'Osage orange,'
he said. 'The stave came up by train
from Texas. It's a fine tree – good
as yew for a self-bow. The heart-
wood's strong and the sapwood's supple.'
We watched the nighthawks for a while,
and he added, 'How I wish you
could have seen him draw it. Eighty
pounds it pulled, maybe eighty-five.
                    Too much for me.'

How he had cared for it, rubbing
it down with resin, checking it
for cracks that could devour its lithe-
some limbs. But he never tested
the fullness of its cast – as if
he feared he'd break *his* back and not
the bow's. And now he was set on
giving it to me... 'So,' he teased,
'You've gone all quiet on me now.
You don't blame me still for selling...'
                    'Don't start,' I said.

'It's over and done with. Let's walk
to the meadow and watch the stars.'
Two hours I lay there as he slept
on his striped horse-blanket, the smell
of arab sweat strong as the crushed
sage and thyme. An owl cried. The half-
moon climbed. Still I saw them: the bear,
the scales, the star-swan, the centaur
with his bow, his arm taut as the
invisible string, his blank eye
                    keen as his aim.

What This Juniper Says About His Mind

I see it now, father, lost
    in falling snow,
the whorl and twist
    of its branches slow

as thought's candelabra. Fire
    hasn't scorched it;
bare roots clutch bare
    rocks; eight unlit

spires pierce the snowbound
    dark. I touch
its bark, and bend
    to hear cold flakes brush

against it, filling cracks
    as grains of sand fill
an hourglass. What sparks
    of memory travel

its branches? What red resin
    perfumes its core?
I see no metaphor – no reason
    to believe that my fear

of your decline can find
    some solace in this tree,
whose two living sprays (found
    tangled in the splay

of green belonging
    to its neighbor) shine
with beauty. Or does my longing
    quicken their sheen?

The Melvina Fire

Between these chimneys, in this air
cleared by fire of all life's clutter,

bare lives were lived. There, near the hearth
sparkling with isinglass, a woman gave birth

to stillborn twins. There, under the roof that dripped
tin tears, her husband kept

his vigil over celestial bodies.
Grief, ornate, dyed dowries;

plates scrubbed of gilt never served
the tongue's luxuries. Love was saved

scrupulously, in mason jars, for lean
seasons, and hope burned quick as grain…

Behind charred barns, garlands
entwine, worn by speculative hands.

Barn Burning, Fall River, Wisconsin, July 1966

Back of the house, past hickory trees and mangled sheets,
stood the barn where my mother swung above the threshing floor,
dared by her brothers, scared by the freight-train rush of air
slamming her chest, her rope-burned hands losing their purchase

as she flew through the dark and fell into my arms. Only in dreams
can I save her like this – her thinness through gingham,
her jujube breath. We lie for years and years as doves moan
in rafters for all she lost: the hushed disasters and alarms.

Through wide-swung doors she led me though the crowd:
the whole town of Fall River gathered there in the July forenoon
to watch the burning of the barn. It was gone by the midday siren.
Boys threw chairs onto its smoldering shade.

Was it progress of a kind to stand with her at childhood's edge,
on fresh asphalt, by the new aluminum garage?
No bats, no memories, no ropes to test her courage –
our Ektachrome smiles gleam like her green crowned Dodge.

Lost Letter to Crane

You said everything you knew about love
you learned from me, Stevie, but that just
ain't true. No mercy, no by-your-leave –
love's war to you. I didn't have the least
little chance, did I baby? I wish you'd caught
malaria on that boat – I wish you'd plum
drowned so you wouldn't be lolling with that fat
madam, the one who owns the Hotel de Dream.
Is that how you want to end your days?
Smoking cigars on a porch in Jacksonville
while she rolls a roulade, whips mayonnaise, says
'I'm tired, honey. Come lay with me for a spell.'

P.S. If you stick even one little lock of my hair
into those lines of yours I'll kill you, I swear.

The Red Tide

Look north, father, to the red tide
sweeping the valley, the great red
tide dyeing the ponderosas, father,
flooding the escarpments where the North
Vrain forks from the South. Look

north, as hawks cross the Cache la Poudre
flowing red through red valleys, its cache
of snow and ice rattling across
black boulders. Look hard, as hawks
look with agate eyes at the north

wind leaping the Divide, sweeping granite
cold across the Medicine Bow, sweeping
red-tinged snow over the divide
between Pacific and Atlantic. Look, as the leaping
deer looks to the woods for safety as the wind

wafts the scent of his pursuer to his flaring
nostrils. Look, as tracks melt and the pursuer
flares into flame, and all he sees with his
melting eyes is fire, and the scent
of fear smokes in him as he burns, and wafts

south in advance of the red tide. Father,
shut your eyes to it – let the tide
reflect in my eyes, not yours: the red's
too strong, the fire's too young, its advance
too quick. Shut your eyes as cinders float south.

Two Ghazals for Aziz, Who Spent Eighteen Years in Darkness in Tazmamart Prison

after Lorca

I

Night everlasting, night unfallen:
You drew it round you, a river swollen.

Mind-slowing cold, cold congealing:
Indigo past depth or feeling.

Time confined, time without measure:
Lives unspent withheld their treasure.

Cells too small to stretch or stand:
Spines recoiled on hard-packed sand.

Bread you gnawed for days and days:
Bread mixed with clay and cockroaches.

Ears attuned to scorpions
Dropped from ceilings: prison's djinns.

Bird-song over years deciphered:
News of rain, and deaths delivered.

Feast of spices, soul's own fire:
Desert vastness sought in prayer.

Tales recalled and tales invented
Twenty starving men enchanted.

II

In your thirteenth year
you dreamed of your release
and your mother in a white dress,
dousing your fever.

Hope pierced you –
a sliver of hope cruel
as Azrael, pale
scyther of souls.

Five more black summers
and you would embrace
her wasted
body, and stroke her hair.

No dream could prepare
you for it: that warrant
of lightness, that torrent
of gladness, that glare.

Romance de la Luna

from Lorca

The moon came to the forge
dragging her train of lilies.
The boy looks and looks –
the boy watches.

In trembling air
the moon waves her arms
and bares, glistening and pure,
her breasts of tin.

Run moon, moon, moon.
If the gypsies come
they will strike from your heart
collars and white rings.

Let me dance, child.
When the gypsies come
they will find you on the anvil
with your eyes closed.

Run moon, moon, moon –
for I hear their horses.
Let me be, child. Don't step
on my starched whiteness.

The horseman drew near,
rattling his tambourine.
Inside the forge
the boy lay, unwatching.

Through olive groves
rode dreams of bronze –
the gypsies. Heads raised,
eyes half-closed.

How the barn-owl calls,
how he calls from the branches!
Across the sky walks the moon,
holding a child by the hand.

Inside the forge the gypsies
weep and wail.
The air watches, watches.
The air keeps vigil.

Romance Sonámbulo

fragments from Lorca

Green I desire you green.
Green wind. Green limbs.
Ship on the sea,
Mare in the mountains.

Waist-deep in shadows,
she broods by the railing.
Green flesh and green hair,
eyes of cold silver.

Green I desire you green.
Under an Andaluz moon
things are watching her
but she cannot see them.

Green I desire you green.
Great stars of frost
arrive with the shadow-fish
that cuts a path to dawn.

Fig-trees chafe the wind
with sandpaper leaves;
hills like thieving cats
bristle with agaves.

Who will come, and from where?
She keeps her vigil –
Green flesh and green hair,
dreams in bitter sea-swell.

False lanterns of tin
trembled on roof-tiles.
A thousand glass tambourines
injured the dawn.

Over the cistern's face
the gypsy girl swayed.
Green flesh and green hair,
eyes of cold silver.

An icicle of moon
suspended her there.
Night grew intimate
like a village square.

Green I desire you green.
Green wind. Green limbs.
Ship on the sea.
Mare in the mountains.

La Monja Gitana

from Lorca

Silence of lime and myrtle.
Mallow in fine grass.
On her fair linen,
scent of wallflowers.

Seven bird-prisms fly
from the pewter chandelier.
The distant church rumbles
like a well-fed bear.

How well she sews!
On the altar shroud,
imagination's petals
slowly unfold.

Sunflowers! Magnolias
of sequins and ribbons!
Saffron-stigmas and moons
adorn fair linen.

Five bitter oranges
ripen on kitchen plate.
In the church of Almería,
five wounds are cut.

In the eyes of the nun
two men ride past.
A final rumour
loosens from her chest.

Frozen, distant –
stone clouds depart.
Scent of verbena –
a cracked sugar-heart.

Twenty suns survey
the upraised plain.
The mind's rivers
stand on end.

She pierces her flowers
while, in the breeze,
high light plays chess
through jalousies.

Reyerta

from Lorca

In the middle of the gorge
lie Albacete's knives,
glazed with contrary blood,
lovely as fish-graves.

Light hard as hearts and aces
cuts from bitter green
profiles of horses
and infuriated men.

Two ancient women weep
in an olive tree's crown.
The quarrel's bull-fury
climbs parapets of stone.

Black angels deliver
snowmelt and white scarves.
Angels with wings
forged from Albacete's knives.

Juan Antonio of Montilla
tumbles to the plain,
his body filled with iris,
head a pomegranate stain.
Now he rides a fiery cross
as death's highwayman.

Flanked by Civil Guards,
the judge rides through olive groves.
A mute song of serpents:
spilt blood cries and seethes.

Esteemed Civil Guards,
it's the same schoolboy lesson.
Here died four Romans
and five Carthaginians.

Fig-trees and hot rumours
goad the afternoon,
which soaks, unconscious,
into the shanks of wounded men.

Black angels soar
through westerly air.
Angels with lubricious hearts
and black braided hair.

Circumspect

She was ravelling, ravelling,
weaving and unweaving
a bright shroud,
her mind travelling
every route and road,
turning and returning
             to his leaving.

She was hunting, hunting,
as a king
pursues the fawn,
her arrows blunting
the doubts she dwelt upon,
turning and returning
             to what he'd done.

She was listening, listening
for a voice
unlike her own,
songbirds hastening
to prove what she'd forgone,
turning and returning
             their harmonies.

She was testing, testing,
searching for
a lover's face,
her love outlasting
every fatal guess,
turning and returning
             their private share.

She was pacing, pacing
in her old prison,
her mind racing
and her work undone,
turning and returning
             to their burning.

Admetus, Alcestis

after Herbert

He strokes her hair,
breathes her beauty,
carries her up the stair
to the bed where she wept for duty,
drops her shroud onto a chair.

What groves
of words, what shadow-lines
save this lover's loves?
What unveiled truth gains
from praise at two removes?

Carpe Diem

Grief saw two quiet children
walking to the palace in Corinth,
carrying gifts for a princess –
a crown, a glittering gown –
and grief, ever-present, living
wholly and invisibly in the present,
let them pass. The very air
trembled as they climbed the steps
to meet their futures, pleased
with the beauty of their gifts,
pleased by the kisses and blessings
lavished on them as they passed.
Grief drew back, and let them enjoy
the moment, and their father's pride.
For he, too, walked by their side,
unknowing, proud of his sons
and his new bride, proud
of the woman who had forgiven him
and made this offering as a token
of her love. Grief sought
itself, safe in the immanent
knowledge that shone like peace
or crowns. Grief looked on,
as it looks on the child in the explosive
vest, or the unconscious crowd in the café,
or the disposing man who holds
his life in his hands with a care
that seems, from a distance,
almost like tenderness.

In Troezen

In Troezen,
before the hanging of a queen,
before the trampling of a virgin
by his own horses, in green
     surf frozen
in a king's memory, this scene
appears: a spring, a fountain,
pools where flocks of women
     rinse crimson
shawls, and spread them on
white rocks under the sun,
in summer's blue oblivion.

Sacrifice

On the mount, the boy, bound
and unwilling, waiting for the wound,
terror-struck by the sound
of his father's breathing, and the blind
thrust of the knife that seemed
to hover in midair, in falling wind.

Near the bay, the girl, unbound
and willing, watching his hand,
mesmerised by the sound
of her father's breathing, and the blind
sweep of the sword that gleamed
in midair, in rising wind.

The scent of forgiveness is not sweet.
On abandoned ground, in moonlight,
charred bones give up their meat.

The Swerve

If a young girl thought that her soul left her as she slept,
drawn out of her body like a letter from a perfumed envelope –
if she believed that the white peach she ate for breakfast had slipped
from a tree in a Nepalese courtyard in the fourteenth century,
would these be fatal errors? If, purely by chance, she chose to hope
that fall would one day rub against spring, or that poles and parentheses
would give up their old hostilities and nestle like spoons,
would this be the first step towards an unholy system of thought?
If she swerves, pursues the firefly's path, ignores the moon's
rectitudes, who will follow her through doubt and danger? Not I,
who discovered her too late; not you, the faceless stranger who
                                                    reads her fate
between these lines and shuts her in darkness, tucks her away.

Snow Is Not Celibate

Snow is not celibate. Its errors, though immense,
are seldom permanent, its indiscrimination
just. Efforts must be made to understand
its point of view. Who can fault its deceptions?
White lies are socially acceptable,
and as for the howlers – well, snow's prone
to exaggeration. Its slide towards disaster
(the blanket denials, the heaped-up scorn)
was hardly a shock. As for that manic streak,
no whisperer, gentle or not, could break it.
Who can change a blizzard's nature? Yet
beneath its fake *froideur* abides a pure
and succouring soul – a soul to melt
the hardest heart, staunch the deepest doubt.

Fixed Form

There's a sliver in my eye.
    My heart is cold.
Children cannot rescue me
    with tears that scald.

Blue auroras light the panes
    of my prison.
Driven crystals pierce my veins
    with precision.

Etched upon an icy lake
    old patterns shine.
Love's reversals cannot make
    their meanings mine.

What malice cramped my hand?
    Who fixed my form?
I wish a lime-scented wind
    would make me warm.

Myth and Muse

Would she be pleased to be excised?
Influence is absence. All hers:
blanks, zeros, blue peninsulas,
dashes and stays. If she's surmised,

let it be by evanescent
routes, distant as mail from Tunis
or extinct colours: amethyst's
vapour, Saturn's adamant.

In the end, it's impossible.
Even here her black-plumed horses
toss their heads. Who can erase
the veiled threat, kill the bride of style?

A Second Moon

Earth may once have had a small second moon that perished in a slow-motion collision with its companion.

the BBC World Service, 3 August 2011

Was there a second moon? Imagine her
suspended above a disbelieving crater –

if she's remarkable no one can tell.
An unperceiving vacuum holds her small

circumference, and unmapped seas
reflect a face that, in circumstances

more favourable to praise, might be called
beautiful. No eyes, wide and wild,

regard her with fear or superstition.
No poet's conceit or paean

distends her features. If she's destined
to disappear, no one regrets the end

of the story. Stars are opposed to tragedy,
and even the moon on which she

spilled herself has no skill for metonym.
Was the sum greater than its parts? To whom

could she display her wounds?
Who could say 'Twice in two blue moons'?

The Best Time to Talk about Neutrinos

The best time to talk about neutrinos
    is between 2 and 3 am,
when the earth's as invisible to us
    as it is to them, and thoughts zoom

like bullets through snow to superluminal
    beauty... In the blue glass by the bed
I see them racing. Outside, in the communal
    gardens, a vixen screams. You turn your head –

are you listening? 'Through the round earth's
    imagin'd corners...' What Donne
could have done with neutrinos! Your breath's
    hot on my neck... Why does a muon

spin left, and an anti-muon spin right?
    Why are some neutrinos sterile, while
others are... Bother. How can I concentrate
    when you're pressing your whole

weight against my side – your right arm's
    pinning me down... I've lost my train
of thought... What charms
    neutrinos? What grand plan

accounts for their flavours
    and fickle behaviour? The bells
of St Paul's strike four; a swan veers
    past, pinions creaking... All's

down to chance – even the way
    you grip my thigh as you sleep,
imagining it's a girl, a tree, a stray
    ship tumbling down a slippery slope:

'Arise, arise, you numberless infinities.'
    A thrush sings. Ends loosen
from their beginnings as you reach for my waist.
    Lamp-posts lean, leaves listen,

light leaps to mind –
    fresh, blinding. From every corner
of the room comes the sound
    of phantom particles. You uncomb my hair…

Merce Cunningham at Craneway, Last Rehearsals, November 2008

Centripetal in your chair,
you watch your dancers
career,
their daring grace

recalling yours
as it once was,
years and agile years
ago – and still is,

though in your mind only.
Light, liquid, glides
through glass; gainly
shadows meet in shades

of brightness; outside,
on the bay, sails
collide,
their patterns mirrored by girls

skimming across the stage
with that randomness
you loved: badinage
of bodies. All's quiet – unless

we count the beat of feet
as music, or the cry of gulls,
or snapping sails, or the slight
thrum of distant diesels.

The score you'll add
later, after your death
perhaps – music made
as the dance was, from breath

and breathing: bellied
like sails, tallied like age
or divining sticks, sallied
onto the soul's stage.

On the Day He Suffered Most, Sycamores

toss like flocks of lapwings, like dolphins
leaping to last light, like the manes

of green horses, like love just beyond his reach,
like the leaves of books he'll never read, or the stretch

of sea where his father left him a moment too long,
and a wave tumbled him into darkness so strong

he couldn't see or hear or breathe… until the seethe
of leaves lifts him – and through the pane, unscathed,

he watches himself slow, settle, cease.

A Glass of Water

(Port-au-Prince, January 2010)

On the third day he found her, crushed,
swollen lips open, teeth
gritty with ash, and ashen too
her brow and matted hair,
pinafore, bare muscular thighs,
bare feet. He carried her
down the cordoned street, survivors
watching them, scarves blotting
their mouths. Urgent talk, shoves, a flash...

How well he judged it, the picture-
taker; how perfectly
right it seems, that moment when her
head lolls, and she reveals
her clay-streaked thigh — so that I, half-
way around the world, think:
'What perfection. No ivory
Christ could be more moving,
no Zurbarán could say as much.'

How seductive, this well-framed truth!
I hold my own scarf to my face,
stare in fascinated horror...
Even the small boy to my right,
the one with the basketball shirt
and bright red-rimmed eyes — even he
seems to say, '*C'est le Mort-vivant
qui se promène ici... J'ai peur,
j'ai peur de Lui.*' Or am I wrong?

Is he saying something simpler?
Could it be: '*C'est pas ma mère, peut-
être elle est encore en vie.*'
Or is he looking not at her
or at the man who carries her
(thin, not young, staggering slightly)
but the photographer? '*Ne la
prenez pas,*' he seems to say, '*Mais
donnez-moi un petit verre d'eau…*'

In Memory of the Photographer Wilson 'Snowflake' Bentley, Who Died of Pneumonia after Walking through a Blizzard Near Jericho, Vermont, December 23, 1931

Beauty was, for him, cold,
hexagonal, perfect
in all its parts, beheld

once and once only. Locked
beneath his lens, light-spun
and light-refracting, flecked

with coal dust and pollen,
his flakes shone with lunar
loveliness... And we can

see, in these hundred-year-
old prints, plain evidence
of his attention, care,

and chilling confidence:
in the manifold world,
its willed evanescence,

its subtle signs and wild
and blinding storms. Did it
surprise him, to be killed

by a surfeit of white –
a blazing increment
of stars, ferns, wands and bright

escutcheons, an argent
army of perfectness?
Look, and see his wind-bent

back, his boots caked with ice,
his glazed eyes... Did he have,
in his last seditious

delirium, one brave
black thought: did God murder
us all with too much love?

Directive

In Memory of the Photographer Tim Hetherington, Killed by a Mortar Blast on the Tripoli Highway in Misrata, 20 April 2011

Come close. Press eye to subject.
Leave no space between the living
and the dead. Make him, the one enduring fact,
the image created from this moment
and no other. As hawthorn's scent
drives spring into the mind, bring this corpse
to consciousness, and make him fill this room,
where gold's gone dim and lapis
            peace hardens... Raise him,
and touch his face. Trace with newest
light the cracked lips and broken capillaries, the contract-
ing pupils... Prove, from his wounds, the force
of love's violence, and say, with emphatic
silence: This is Christ. This is not Christ.

Notes

Bob-Mill: Fustian is a heavy cloth of twill or napped cotton. Many mills in West Yorkshire, where this poem is set, specialised in the making of it.

The White Horse: The White Horse of Uffington, carved into a scarp in the Berkshire Downs, is at least 3,000 years old. Its bold abstractions resolve themselves only when the figure is seen from a distance.

Rievaulx I and II: Founded in the Yorkshire Dales in the twelfth century and dissolved on the orders of Henry VIII in 1538, Rievaulx was the first Cistercian abbey in the north of England. Aelred was its third abbot.

Whistler at Midnight contains a line from Baudelaire's 'Le Crépuscule du soir.' The pleasure-gardens of Cremorne, frequented by London's demi-monde and by Whistler, Swinburne, and Dante Gabriel Rossetti, were closed in 1877.

Love-Sonnet to a Rock in Bohuslän: *Rönn* is the Swedish word for rowan. *Kist* is the Gaelic word for chest (*kista* in Swedish).

Lost Letter to Crane: Stephen Crane narrowly survived the sinking of the *Commodore* in 1897 (subject of his story 'The Open Boat'). Later that year, he and his wife Cora travelled to Greece, where both worked as war correspondents. A bold (and undervalued) writer of verse, Crane called his poems 'lines'.

Two Ghazals for Aziz are modelled after Federico García Lorca's 'Gacela de la Terrible Presencia' and 'Gacela del Amor Desesperado'. The story of Aziz BineBine and his imprisonment is recounted in the novel *This Blinding Absence of Light* by Tahar Ben Jelloun and in BineBine's memoir *Tazmamort*.

La Monja Gitana: 'Fair linen' is the name of the third, uppermost layer of cloth laid on the altar in Roman Catholic churches. It symbolises the shroud of Christ, and is embroidered with five crosses – one in each corner and one in the centre – signifying the five stigmata.

Admetus, Alcestis: The end-rhymes of this lyric are taken from George Herbert's poem 'Jordan (I)'.

Carpe Diem: In Euripides' tragedy, Medea sends her two sons with poisoned gifts for her husband's new wife. The first line of the poem is a paraphrase of the first line of Robert Frost's 'Carpe Diem'.

In Troezen: Euripides' play *Hippolytus*, which describes Phaedra's fatal love for her husband's son, takes place in Troezen, a town in the Peloponnesos.

Sacrifice: Whether Iphigenia submitted willingly to her sacrifice is the topic of endless debate. Euripides, in both of his plays about her, implies that she was not coerced – and that her precipitous rescue by Artemis was not anticipated by her father.

Myth and Muse contains two phrases from Emily Dickinson's 'A Route of Evanescence'.

Merce Cunningham at Craneway borrows images from Tacita Dean's *Craneway Event* (2010) a documentary of the last three days of rehearsals of a Cunningham piece performed in the disused Ford motor assembly plant overlooking San Francisco Bay.